CONTENTS

Charlie Munger: In Pursuit of Worldy Wisdom	1
Preface	2
About Charlie Munger	3
Timeline	6
Focus	7
Attention Span & Multi-Tasking	8
Know Thyself	10
Do The Easy Thing	11
Expectation	12
Planning	13
Daily Routines	14
Rationality	15
Sitting and Thinking	16
Stupidity & Overconfidence	17
Admit Failure	18
Forecasting	19
Herd Mentality	20
Circle of Competence	21
Mental Models	23
Misjudgement	25
Lollapalooza Effect	27

Psychological Biases 29
Sperm & Ideas 31
Know What To Avoid 32
Know What's Knowable 38
Know When To Fold 39
Opportunity Cost 40
Self Pity 42
Be Deserving 43
Learn The Big Ideas 44
Inversion 46
Checklists 48
Six-Element System 49
Decision-Making 51
Rationality 53
Good Businesses 54
Dealing With Pain 55
The Right People 57
Eminent Dead 59
Marriage 60
Happiness I 61
Opinions 62
Idea Destruction 63
Career 64
Investing 66
Seize The Opportunity 69
Getting Rich 72
Pari-Mutuel Betting 73
Empires 76

Cultivate Learning 77
Civilization 79
Envy 81
Self-Pity 83
China 84
Alibaba 86
Apple 87
Japan 88
Singapore 89
Newspapers 90
Cryptos 91
Speculation & Gambling 93
Gaming 96
Margin Debt 97
Inflation 98
The Great Depression Era 100
Capitalism's Tendency 102
Fund Managers 104
Diversification 105
AntiTrust 106
Energy 107
Global Warming 111
Covid & Vaccine 112
The Great Resignation 114
Timing Markets 115
Happiness II 116
Munger's Book Recommendations 118
Super Investor Series 120

CHARLIE MUNGER: IN PURSUIT OF WORLDY WISDOM

Rui Zhi Dong © 2022

PREFACE

I've been taking notes on Charlie Munger for the last 18 years or so in an attempt to internalize much of the golden nuggets he's shared and to gain a better understanding of how he thinks.

These notes have been built from my attendance at Berkshire Hathaway meetings, Berkshire's annual reports, talks, interviews and Q&As that Munger has given at universities, Wesco, and the Daily Journal Corporation, and from books generally such as *Poor Charlie's Almanack*, *Damn Right!*, and *Seeking Wisdom*.

Each time I review his principles, I gain a new and deeper understanding from his timeless wisdom. I've found Charlie's life philosophy to be incredibly valuable and I hope that you will enjoy them as much as I have.

This book has been organized in a way to give you easy access to Charlie's unique perspective into life by dividing them into byte-sized chunks so that you can come back over and over again for some Munger wisdom.

ABOUT CHARLIE MUNGER

Charlie Munger is best known for being Warren Buffett's right-hand man at Berkshire Hathaway.

Whereas Warren Buffett is known for being single-mindedly focused on investing, Charlie Munger has a very broad range of interests and his tastes eclectic.

Like Warren Buffett, Charlie Munger also wanted to get rich. Not because he wanted fast cars but because he craved independence.

He found it undignified to have to send invoices to people when he was working as a lawyer. He also found some of the clients he worked with to be somewhat unsavory characters and that law wasn't going to be a path to wealth. Thus began his journey into investments.

He one time said that he wanted a lot of children, a house with lots of books, and enough money to have freedom.

Most of his education is self-taught. He learns best by reading through all of the materials alone. He's said on multiple occasions that he prefers learning from the eminent dead than from living teachers.

His kids called him a book with a couple of legs sticking out.

Munger can be quite impulsive and typifies the absent-minded professor. Buffett was one time walking with Charlie in New York talking about a business deal.

Then suddenly Buffett realized he was talking to himself.

Charlie had disappeared.

It turned out that Munger remembered he had a plane to catch and simply walked off.

"I'm always thinking about other things. I forget to look around."

Originally trained as a meteorologist during World War II and then as lawyer at Harvard, Charlie Munger met Warren Buffett in 1959 at a dinner party and the pair immediately hit it off.

Buffett later manager to convince Munger to get into investing and the two have remained close ever since.

Munger later joined Berkshire Hathaway as vice chairman in 1978.

Bill Gates once said of Charlie Munger:

He is truly the broadest thinker I have ever encountered.

From business principles to economic principles to the design of student dormitories to the design of a catamaran he has no equal.

Our longest correspondence was a detailed discussion on the mating habits of naked mole rats and what the human species might learn from them.

Warren Buffett on Munger:

He marches to the beat of his own music, and it's music like virtually no one else is listening to.

TIMELINE

1924: Born in Omaha, Nebraska

1959: Meets Warren Buffett

1962-1975: Runs Wheeler, Munger and Company, an investment firm

1965: Stops practicing law

1978 - Present: Vice Chairman of Berkshire Hathaway

FOCUS

Our job is to find a few intelligent things to do, not to keep up with every damn thing in the world.

Even bright people are going to have limited, really valuable insights in a very competitive world when they're fighting against other very bright, hardworking people.

And it makes sense to load up on the very few good insights you have instead of pretending to know everything about everything at all times.

ATTENTION SPAN & MULTI-TASKING

I think people who multi-task pay a huge price.

They think they're being extra productive, and I think they're out of their mind. I use the metaphor of the one-legged man in the ass-kicking contest.

If you don't know how to think, you'll always be a one-legged man in an ass kicking contest.

I think when you multi-task so much, you don't have time to think about anything deeply.

You're giving the world an advantage you shouldn't do.

Practically everybody is drifting into that mistake.

Concentrating hard on something is important. I can't succeed at all without doing it. I did not succeed in life by intelligence. I succeeded because I have a long attention span.

A long attention span will help you a lot if you're reasonably smart.

If you're reasonably obsessed with something, even if it's

intermittent, and you have a long attention span, you keep working over the serious problems, then you'll stumble into an answer.

KNOW THYSELF

Knowing what you don't know is more useful than being brilliant.

Always act within your circle of competence.

If you have competence, you know the edge. It wouldn't be a competence if you didnt know where the boundaries lie.

Asking whether you've passed the boundary is a question that almost answers itself.

We have to have a special insight, or we'll put it in the 'too tough' basket. All of you have to look for a special area of competency and focus on that.

DO THE EASY THING

My idea of shooting a fish in a barrel is draining the barrel first.

We're the tortoise that has outrun the hare because it chose the easy predictions.

The more hard lessons you can learn vicariously rather than through your own hard experience, the better.

EXPECTATION

People need to ask, "How do I play the hand that has been dealt me?"

The world is not going to give you extra return just because you want it.

You have to be very shrewd and hard working to get a little extra. It's so much easier to reduce your wants. There are a lot of smart people and a lot of them cheat, so it's not easy to win.

PLANNING

At Berkshire there has never been a master plan. Anyone who wanted to do it, we fired because it takes on a life of its own and doesn't cover new reality.

We want people taking into account new information.

DAILY ROUTINES

I like to fulfill my duties first because I don't want to disappoint people. But I say no to many new opportunities.

Munger generally keeps an open calendar like Buffett. He likes to have the freedom to take calls from friends and family. He doesn't want to be booked like a busy doctor.

RATIONALITY

I think that one should recognize reality even when one doesn't like it; indeed, especially when one doesn't like it.

Your life must focus on the maximization of objectivity.

Rationality is not just something you do so that you can make more money, it is a binding principle.

Rationality is a really good idea. You must avoid the nonsense that is conventional in one's own time. It requires developing systems of thought that improve your batting average over time.

I think scientific literacy is terribly important. Habits of the mind formed from science are so valuable. Even if you're not a scientist, you can pick up on the big ideas like thermodynamics. A lot of people haven't bothered to learn thermodynamics, and that's a big mistake.

I almost worship reason. You can argue that Henry Singleton did too and certainly Warren Buffett.

SITTING AND THINKING

For many people it's good that they're extra busy.

They're not good thinkers, so you get more out of them if they just keep doing what they're doing.

But if you're a person of good cognition, you can learn a lot more if you put your mind to it. I don't think there's any substitute for just sitting and thinking.

STUPIDITY & OVERCONFIDENCE

It's remarkable how much long-term advantage people like us have gotten by trying to be consistently not stupid, instead of trying to be very intelligent. There must be some wisdom in the folk saying: "It's the strong swimmers who drown"

A strong swimmer, being overly confident, tends to take more risks and go swimming where nature can be stronger than them.

The harder you work, the more confidence you get. But you may be working hard on something that is false.

I try to get rid of people who always confidently answer questions about which they don't have any real knowledge.

ADMIT FAILURE

Acknowledging what you don't know is the dawning of wisdom.

I like people admitting they were complete stupid horses' asses. I know I'll perform better if I rub my nose in my mistakes. This is a wonderful trick to learn.

It's a good habit to trumpet your failures and be quiet about your successes.

FORECASTING

People have always had this craving to know the future.

The King used to hire the magician or the forecaster and he'd look in sheep guts or something for an answer as to how to handle the next war and so there's always been a market for people who reported to know the future based on their expertise.

There's a lot of that still going on.

It's just as crazy as when the king was hiring the forecaster who looked at the sheep guts and people have an economic incentive to sell.

HERD MENTALITY

A teacher asks her class a question:

There are ten sheep in a pen. If one jumps out then how many are left?

All said 9, except one who said there would be none left.

The teacher said, "obviously, you don't understand math."

The student replied, "no, you don't understand sheep."

CIRCLE OF COMPETENCE

I'm no genius. I'm smart in spots—but I stay around those spots. — Tom Watson Sr., Founder of IBM

There are a lot of things we pass on.

We have three baskets: In, Out and Too Tough.

A lot of stuff goes into the *Too Tough* basket.

We can't do that if it's a problem at a Berkshire subsidiary company, but if we don't own it, we just pass.

I don't know how people cope trying to figure everything out.

We have to have a special insight, or we'll put it in the *Too Tough* basket. All of you have to look for a special area of competency and focus on that.

You have to figure out what your own aptitudes are.

If you play games where other people have the aptitudes and you don't, you're going to lose.

And that's as close to certain as any prediction that you can make.

You have to figure out where you've got an edge. And you've got to play within your own circle of competence.

If you want to be the best tennis player in the world, you may start out trying and soon find out that it's hopeless -- that other people blow right by you.

However, if you want to become the best plumbing contractor in Bemidji, that is probably doable by two-thirds of you.

It takes a will. It takes the intelligence. But after a while, you'd gradually know all about the plumbing business in Bemidji and master the art.

That is an attainable objective, given enough discipline.

And people who could never win a chess tournament or stand in center court in a respectable tennis tournament can rise quite high in life by slowly developing a circle of competence—which results partly from what they were born with and partly from what they slowly develop through work.

MENTAL MODELS

Developing the habit of mastering the multiple models which underlie reality is the best thing you can do.

If you skillfully follow the multidisciplinary path, you will never wish to come back. It would be like cutting off your hands.

The first rule is that you can't really know anything if you just remember isolated facts and try and bang 'em back.

If the facts don't hang together on a latticework of theory, you don't have them in a usable form.

You've got to have models in your head. And you've got to array your experience -- both vicarious and direct -- on this latticework of models.

You may have noticed students who just try to remember and pound back what is remembered. Well, they fail in school and in life.

You've got to hang experience on a latticework of models in your head.

You need a different checklist and different mental models for different companies.

I can never make it easy by saying, *Here are three things.*

You have to derive it yourself to ingrain it in your head for the rest of your life.

Have a full kit of tools, go through them in your mind checklist-style.

The only antidote for being an absolute klutz due to the presence of a man with a hammer syndrome is to have a full kit of tools.

MISJUDGEMENT

I suppose it is tempting, if the only tool you have is a hammer, to treat everything as if it were a nail. — Abraham Maslow

You know the old saying -- to the man with a hammer, the world looks like a nail. This is a dumb way of handling problems.

Misjudgment is like sunshine, it will always be part of the world. Many of the misjudgments will be massive. We have misjudgment too at Berkshire, but we have less than others. If you can stay high in the pack, you'll do well.

The best chapter in *Outliers* was about people with an IQ of 200 who failed utterly in life. If you can't learn from that chapter, I don't want to bet on you. I don't know Gladwell but I was flabbergasted – it was a marvelous book. It gives you an insight into what you might call fate. It is good to know how fate will rule your odds.

My favorite human misjudgment is self-serving bias -- how the brain will subconsciously decide that what is good for the holder of the brain is good for everyone else. *If the little me wants it, why shouldn't the little me have it?*

People go through life like this. I've underestimated this phenomenon all my life. People go bonkers taking care of their own self-interest. It's a sea of miscognition.

People who write the laws, people who treat patients, who experiment with rats, all suffer horribly from this bias.

LOLLAPALOOZA EFFECT

What Munger means by Lollapalooza is when you have a few mental models acting in unison, the results are much bigger than the sum of their parts. He takes elements from his study of complex systems and non-linear dynamics. A Lollapalooza in knowledge can be reached such that the results become incredibly beneficial to your decision making.

You get Lollapalooza effects when two, three or four forces are all operating in the same direction. And, frequently, you don't get simple addition.

It's often like a critical mass in physics where you get a nuclear *explosion* if you get to a certain point of mass -- and you don't get anything much worth seeing if you don't reach the mass.

Sometimes the forces just add like ordinary quantities and sometimes they combine on a break-point or critical-mass basis. More commonly, the forces coming out of models are conflicting to some extent. And you get huge, miserable trade-offs, so you must have the models and you must see the relatedness and the effects from the relatedness.

I coined it when I realized I didn't know psychology.

I bought three comprehensive psychology textbooks and read through them, and like usual I thought they were doing it all wrong, and I could do it better.

When three or four tendencies were operating at once in same situation, the outcome wasn't linear, it was straight up.

The scholars were ignoring the most important thing in the profession because they couldn't do experiments with so many variable operating together, and then they didn't synthesize it with other disciplines, because they didn't know squat about other disciplines. I am lonely, but I am right.

PSYCHOLOGICAL BIASES

Hardly anything could be more important to the study of law than the study of psychology, but there's a taboo against it.

There's a lot of miscognition. If you can just tune out all of the big folly, you'd be surprised how well you can do. There's a lot of nuttiness in the world.

You see many people who've gotten straight A's at law school, but they screw up in dealing with self-serving bias.

I would say that the current head of the World Bank, Paul Wolfowitz, had an elementary question -- as head of the World Bank, a lot of people hate you, so how bright do you have to be to distance yourself from a question of a large raise from your live-in girlfriend?

He sent it to the lawyers, they hemmed and hawed, and he lost his moorings. Even a child shouldn't make his obvious mistake. Similarly, I'd guess President Clinton would have had a better record if he'd had better insight on certain subjects.

I once asked a doctor why he was still doing an obsolete cataract operation when a new, better one had been developed. He said, "Because it's so wonderful to teach!"

He only changed when patients voted with their feet. And this was at one of the best medical schools.

Who gives up an operation he likes doing and is really good at? It's a really human thing to cling to things most practiced.

This happens even in physics. A lot of people cling to bad ideas. If the brightest people in the world do this, imagine everyone else.

SPERM & IDEAS

What I'm saying here is that the human mind is a lot like the human egg, and the human egg has a shut-off device.

When one sperm gets in, it shuts down so the next one can't get in. The human mind has a big tendency of the same sort.

And here again, it doesn't just catch ordinary mortals; it catches the deans of physics. According to Max Planck, the really innovative, important new physics was never really accepted by the old guard.

Instead a new guard came along that was less brain-blocked by its previous conclusions. And if Max Planck's crowd had this consistency and commitment tendency that kept their old inclusions intact in spite of disconfirming evidence, you can imagine what the crowd that you and I are part of behaves like.

KNOW WHAT TO AVOID

A lot of success in life and business comes from knowing what you want to avoid: early death, a bad marriage, etc.

I invert. I try to figure out what I don't like and try to avoid it. It's worked wonders for me.

I always say I want to know where I would die so I never go there.

If you have a defect you try to increase, you're on your way to the shallows.

Envy, huge self-pity, extreme ideology, intense loyalty to a particular identity — you've just taken your brain and started to pound on it with a hammer.

Mozart is a good example of a life ruined by nuttiness. His achievement wasn't diminished – he may well have had the best innate musical talent ever – but from that start, he was pretty miserable. He overspent his income his entire life – that will make you miserable.

He was consumed with envy and jealousy of other people who were treated better than he felt they deserved, and he was filled with self-pity. Nothing could be stupider. Even if your child is dying of cancer, it's not okay to feel self pity.

In general, it's totally nonproductive to get the idea that the world is unfair.

Envy is a really stupid sin because it's the only one you could never possibly have any fun at.

There's a lot of pain and no fun. Why would you want to get on that trolley?

One idea is that whenever you think something or some person is ruining your life, it's you. A victimization mentality is so debilitating.

Marcus Aurelius had the notion that every tough stretch was an opportunity. To learn, to display manhood — you name it. To him, it was as natural as breathing to have tough stretches.

Warren doesn't spend any time on self-pity, envy, and so on.

[Johnny] Carson's prescriptions for sure misery included:

1) Ingesting chemicals in an effort to alter mood or perception;

2) Envy;

3) Resentment

I can still recall Carson's absolute conviction as he told how he had tried these things on occasion after occasion, and had become miserable every time.

It is easy to understand Carson's first prescription for misery — ingesting chemicals. I add my voice. The four closest friends of my youth were highly intelligent, ethical, humorous types, favored in person and background.

Two are long dead, with alcohol a contributing factor, and a third is a living alcoholic — if you call that living. While susceptibility varies, addiction can happen to any of us, through a subtle process where the bonds of degradation are too light to be felt until they are too strong to be broken.

And I have yet to meet anyone, in over six decades of life, whose life was worsened by over-fear and over-avoidance of such a deceptive pathway to destruction.

Envy, of course, joins chemicals in winning some sort of quantity price for causing misery.

It was wreaking havoc long before it got a bad press in the laws of Moses.

If you wish to retain the contribution of envy to misery, I recommend that you never read any of the biographies of that good Christian, Samuel Johnson, because his life demonstrates in an enticing way the possibility and advantage of transcending envy.

Resentment has always worked for me exactly as it worked for Carson. I cannot recommend it highly enough to you if you desire misery.

Johnson spoke well when he said that life is hard enough to swallow without squeezing in the bitter rind of resentment.

◆ ◆ ◆

Prescriptions For Misery

First, be unreliable.

Do not faithfully do what you have engaged to do. If you will only master this one habit, you will more than counterbalance the combined effect of all your virtues, howsoever great.

If you like being distrusted and excluded from the best human contribution and company, this prescription is for you. Master this one habit and you can always play the role of the hare in the fable, except that instead of being outrun by one fine turtle you will be outrun by hordes and hordes of mediocre turtles and even by some mediocre turtles on crutches.

My second prescription for misery is to learn everything you possibly can from your own personal experience, minimizing what you learn vicariously from the good and bad experiences of others, living and dead. This prescription is a sure-shot producer of misery and second-rate achievement.

You can see the results of not learning from others' mistakes by simply looking about you. How little originality there is in the common disasters of mankind — drunk driving deaths, reckless driving maimings, incurable venereal diseases, conversion of bright college students into brainwashed zombies as members of destructive cults, business failures through repetition of obvious mistakes made by predecessors, various forms of crowd folly, and so on.

The other aspect of avoiding vicarious wisdom is the rule for not learning from the best work done before yours. The prescription is to become as non-educated as you reasonable can.

My third prescription for misery is to go down and stay down when you get your first, second, third severe reverse in the battle of life.

Because there is so much adversity out there, even for the lucky and wise, this will guarantee that, in due course, you will be permanently mired in misery.

Ignore at all cost the lesson contained in the accurate epitaph written for himself by Epictetus: "Here lies Epictetus, a slave, maimed in body, the ultimate in poverty, and favored by Gods."

My final prescription to you for a life of fuzzy thinking and infelicity is to ignore a story they told me when I was very young about a rustic who said, "I wish I knew where I was going to die, and then I'd never go there."

Most people smile as you did at the rustic's ignorance and ignore his basic wisdom. If my experience is any guide, the rustic's approach is to be avoided at all cost by someone bent on misery.

To help fail you should discount as mere quirk with no useful message the method of the rustic, which is the same one used in Carson's speech.

KNOW WHAT'S KNOWABLE

It's stupid the way people extrapolate the past -- and not slightly stupid, but massively stupid.

We're emphasizing the knowable by predicting how certain people and companies will swim against the current. We're not predicting the fluctuation in the current.

KNOW WHEN TO FOLD

Life, in part, is like a poker game, wherein you have to learn to quit sometimes when holding a much-loved hand—you must learn to handle mistakes and new facts that change the odds.

What you have to learn is to fold early when the odds are against you, or if you have a big edge, back it heavily because you don't get a big edge often.

Opportunity comes, but it doesn't come often, so seize it when it does come.

OPPORTUNITY COST

Intelligent people make decisions based on opportunity costs.

I just wanted to do the best I could reasonably do with the talent, time and resources I had available.

That's what I was doing then and now. Everything is based on opportunity costs.

Academia has done a terrible disservice. They teach in one sentence in first-year economics about opportunity costs, but that's it. In life, if opportunity A is better than B, and you have only one opportunity, you do A.

There's no one size fits all. If you're really wise and fortunate, you get to be like Berkshire. We have high opportunity costs. We always have something we like and can buy more of, so that's what we compare everything to.

When someone presented a company in an emerging market to Warren Buffett, Warren said, "I don't feel more comfortable about buying this than I feel about adding to our position in Wells Fargo."

He thinks highly of the company and the managers. He was using this as his opportunity cost. He was saying, "Don't talk about anything unless it's better than buying more Wells Fargo."

It doesn’t matter to Warren where the opportunity is. He has no preconceived ideas about whether Berkshire’s money ought to be in this or that. He’s scanning the world trying to get his opportunity cost as high as he can so his individual decisions would be better.

Opportunity cost is a huge filter in life. If you've got two suitors who are really eager to have you and one is way the hell better than the other, you do not have to spend much time with the other.

And that's the way we filter out buying opportunities.

SELF PITY

You do not want to drift into self-pity. I had a friend who carried a thick stack of linen-based cards. And when somebody would make a comment that reflected self-pity, he would slowly and portentously pull out his huge stack of cards, take the top one and hand it to the person. The card said, "Your story has touched my heart. Never have I heard of anyone with as many misfortunes as you."

Self-pity is always counterproductive. It's the wrong way to think. And when you avoid it, you get a great advantage over everybody else because self pity is a standard response. And you can train yourself out of it.

Whenever you think something or some person is ruining your life, it's you.

A victimization mentality is so debilitating.

BE DESERVING

The safest way to get what you want is to deserve what you want.

The iron rule of nature is: you get what you reward for. If you want ants to come, you put sugar on the floor.

LEARN THE BIG IDEAS

I think you should be intelligent in improving yourself.

All the big ideas in every discipline are very useful.

You're way better to take on a really big, important idea that comes up all the time than some little tiny idea you may not face.

Master the best that other people have ever figured out. I don't believe in just sitting down and trying to dream it all up yourself. Nobody's that smart.

If we are to understand how the world really works, we need to understand the big ideas and how they work. Most problems we struggle with can be solved by reaching into another discipline.

I think scientific literacy is terribly important.

Habits of the mind formed from science are so valuable.
Even if you're not a scientist, you can pick up on the big ideas like thermodynamics. A lot of people haven't bothered to learn thermodynamics, and that's a big mistake.

What I noted since the really big ideas carry 95% of the freight, it wasn't at all hard for me to pick up all the big ideas from all the big disciplines and make them a standard part of my mental routines.

Once you have the ideas, of course, they are no good if you don't practice — if you don't practice you lose it.

So I went through life constantly practicing this model of the multidisciplinary approach. Well, I can't tell you what that's done for me. It's made life more fun, it's made me more constructive, it's made me more helpful to others, it's made me enormously rich, you name it, that attitude really helps.

Now there are dangers there, because it works so well, that if you do it, you will frequently find you are sitting in the presence of some other expert, maybe even an expert that's superior to you, supervising you. And you will know more than he does about his own specialty, a lot more. You will see the correct answer when he's missed it.

It doesn't help you just to know them enough just so you can give them back on an exam and get an A. You have to learn these things in such a way that they're in a mental latticework in your head and you automatically use them for the rest of your life.

INVERSION

The way complex adaptive systems work and the way mental constructs work, problems frequently get easier and I would even say usually are easier to solve if you turn around in reverse.

In other words, if you want to help India, the question you should ask is not "how can I help India?"

You think, "what's doing the worst damage in India? What would automatically do the worst damage and how do I avoid it?"

You'd think they are logically the same thing, but they're not.

Those of you who have mastered algebra know that inversion frequently will solve problems which nothing else will solve.

And in life, unless you're more gifted than Einstein, inversion will help you solve problems that you can't solve in other ways.

It is not enough to think problems through forward.

You must also think in reverse, much like the rustic who wanted to know where he was going to die so that he'd never go there.

That is why the great algebraist, Carl Jacobi, so often said: "invert, always invert."

And why Pythagoras thought in reverse to prove that the square root of two was an irrational number.

CHECKLISTS

I'm a great believer in solving hard problems by using a checklist.

You need to get all the likely and unlikely answers before you, otherwise it's easy to miss something important.

You need to have appropriate mental models and a checklist to go through each of them.

If 2-3 items are not on the checklist, and you're a pilot, you might crash.

SIX-ELEMENT SYSTEM

Munger on what we can learn from a pilot's training system.

1. His formal education is wide enough to cover practically everything useful in piloting.

2. His knowledge of practically everything needed by pilots is not taught just well enough to enable him to pass one test or two; instead, all of his knowledge is raised to practice-based fluency, even in handling two or three intertwined hazards at once.

3. Like any good algebraist, he is made to think sometimes in a forward fashion and sometimes in reverse; and so he learns when to concentrate mostly on what he wants to happen and also when to concentrate mostly on avoiding what he does not want to happen.

4. His training time is allocated among subjects so as to minimize damage from his later malfunctions; and so what is most important in his performance gets the most training coverage and is raised to the highest fluency levels.

5. "Checklist" routines are always mandatory for him

6. Even after original training he is forced into a special knowledge-maintenance routine through the regular use of the aircraft simulator to prevent atrophy through long disuse of skills

needed to cope with rare and important problems.

The need for this clearly correct six-element system, with its large demands in a narrow-scale field where stakes are high, is rooted in the deep structure of the human mind.

Therefore, we must expect that the education we need for broad scale problem-solving will keep all these elements but with awesomely expanded coverage for each element.

DECISION-MAKING

Personally, I've gotten so that I now use a kind of two-track analysis.

First, what are the factors that really govern the interests involved, rationally considered?

And second, what are the subconscious influences where the brain at a subconscious level is automatically doing these things-which by and large are useful, but which often misfunction.

One approach is rationality — the way you'd work out a bridge problem. By evaluating the real interests, the real probabilities and so forth.

And the other is to evaluate the psychological factors that cause subconscious conclusions — many of which are wrong.

You know what Rudyard Kipling said? Treat those two imposters just the same — success and failure. Of course, there's going to be some failure in making the correct decisions. Nobody bats a thousand. I think it's important to review your past stupidities so you are less likely to repeat them, but I'm not gnashing my teeth over it or suffering or enduring it.

I regard it as perfectly normal to fail and make bad decisions.

I think the tragedy in life is to be so timid that you don't play hard enough so you have some reverses.

RATIONALITY

Your life must focus on the maximization of objectivity.

Rationality is not just something you do so that you can make more money, it is a binding principle.

You must avoid the nonsense that is conventional in one's own time. It requires developing systems of thought that improve your batting average over time.

GOOD BUSINESSES

The difference between a good business and a bad business is that good businesses throw up one easy decision after another.

The bad businesses throw up painful decisions time after time.

DEALING WITH PAIN

Life is always going to hurt some people in some ways and help others. There should be more willingness to take the blows of life as they fall. That's what manhood is, taking life as it falls. Not whining all the time and trying to fix it by whining.

There's danger in just shoveling out money to people who say, 'My life is a little harder than it used to be.' At a certain place you've got to say to the people, 'Suck it in and cope, buddy. Suck it in and cope.'

When it comes to adversity, you have just to soldier through. Being too frightened leads to contempt. Coping with adversity brings opportunities. Don't panic or go crazy. People will always remember the person who could keep his or her cool.

When Bobby Kennedy was dying and the entire Kennedy family was falling apart, Jackie Kennedy was the only person who kept her head.

Who do we remember?

We remember Jackie Kennedy.

I think the attitude of Epictetus is the best.

He thought that every missed chance in life was an opportunity to behave well, every missed chance in life was an opportunity to learn something, and that your duty was not to be submerged in self-pity, but to utilize the terrible blow in constructive fashion.

That is a very good idea.

THE RIGHT PEOPLE

This is a good life lesson: getting the right people into your system is the most important thing you can do.

It's just so useful dealing with people you can trust and getting all the others the hell out of your life. It ought to be taught as a catechism. But wise people want to avoid other people who are just total rat poison, and there are a lot of them.

We try to operate in a web of seamless trust, deserved trust, and try to be careful whom we let in.

We get rid of the craziness, of people checking to make sure it's done right.

The highest form that civilization can reach is a seamless web of deserved trust—not much procedure, just totally reliable people correctly trusting one another.

That's the way an operating room works at the Mayo Clinic.

If a bunch of lawyers were to introduce a lot of process, the patients would all die. So never forget when you're a lawyer that you may be rewarded for selling this stuff but you don't have to buy it.

In your own life what you want is a seamless web of deserved trust. And if your proposed marriage contract has forty-seven pages, I suggest you not enter.

EMINENT DEAD

A second idea that I got very early was that there is no love that's so right as admiration-based love, and that love should include the instructive dead. Somehow, I got that idea and I lived with it all my life; and it's been very, very useful to me.

And I think when you're trying to teach the great concepts that work, it helps to tie them into the lives and personalities of the people who developed them. I think you learn economics better if you make Adam Smith your friend.

That sounds funny, making friends among the eminent dead, but if you go through life making friends with the eminent dead who had the right ideas, I think it will work better in life and work better in education. It's way better than just being given the basic concepts.

MARRIAGE

The best way to get a good spouse is to deserve a good spouse because a good spouse is by definition not nuts.

Ben Franklin gave the best advice which is to keep your eyes wide open before marriage and half shut thereafter.

All honorable people will do the best they can with the
bed they've made. Franklin did that and did not allow himself to feel regret. All in all, he had a fabulous life.

In marriage, you shouldn't look for someone with good looks and character. You look for someone with low expectations.

HAPPINESS I

The secret to happiness is to lower your expectations --that is what you compare your experience with.

If your expectations and standards are very high and only allow yourself to be happy when things are exquisite, you'll never be happy and grateful.

There will always be some flaw. But compare your experience with lower expectations, especially something not as good, and you'll find much in your experience of the world to love, cherish and enjoy, every single moment.

Someone will always be getting richer faster than you. This is not a tragedy.

OPINIONS

It's bad to have an opinion you're proud of if you can't state the arguments for the other side better than your opponents.

This is a great mental discipline.

I have what I call an iron prescription that helps me keep sane when I naturally drift toward preferring one ideology over another and that is: I say that I'm not entitled to have an opinion on this subject unless I can state the arguments against my position better than the people who support it.

I think only when I've reached that state am I qualified to speak. This business of not drifting into extreme ideology is a very, very important thing in life.

IDEA DESTRUCTION

Any year that passes in which you don't destroy one of your best loved ideas is a wasted year.

We all are learning, modifying, or destroying ideas all the time. Rapid destruction of your ideas when the time is right is one of the most valuable qualities you can acquire. You must force yourself to consider arguments on the other side.

Darwin paid particular attention to disconfirming evidence. Objectivity maintenance routines are totally required in life if you're going to be a great thinker.

CAREER

Three rules for a career: Don't sell anything you wouldn't buy yourself. Don't work for anyone you don't respect and admire. Work only with people you enjoy.

During Charlie Munger's days as a lawyer, he asked himself, 'Who is my most valuable client?' He decided that it was himself. So he decided to sell himself an hour each day.

This became his a daily routine where he spent an hour early in the morning for himself, working on his construction projects and real estate deals. Be the client, then work for other people. In other words, sell yourself an hour a day.

I said I would sell the best hour of the day to myself in order to improve myself. Only then would I sell the rest of my time to my clients. Of course, when I was in a demanding situation, I'd make an exception.

Extreme specialization is the way to succeed. Most people are way better off specializing than trying to understand the world.
A man is a prisoner of his talents.

I have never succeeded very much in anything in which I was not very interested. If you can't somehow find yourself very interested in something, I don't think you'll succeed very much, even if you're fairly smart.

You have to choose something you like doing. I have never been good at things I wasn't interested in.

If you have a passion for drawing buildings then you have to be an architect—which is a terrible way to make money by the way. However, I have an architect friend who says he doesn't care if it is a bad way to make money. The man doesn't care because in his mind it isn't work.

We don't like trading agony for money.

Choose clients as you would friends.

Never abuse current clients by trying to get new ones.
Think how this would work with matrimony – if you ignore your current wife while you pursue another one.

Figure out what you're bad at, and avoid all of it.

We've never succeeded at anything that didn't interest us. And we've never succeeded at anything that was really hard or we didn't have much aptitude for.

It's been my experience in life if you just keep thinking and reading, you don't have to work.

INVESTING

If I were young and had a small amount to invest, I would be looking in the small-cap world.

I wouldn't go where the big boys have to be, trying to decide whether Merck's pipeline is better than Pfizer's.

I'd go where there are market inefficiencies and your work could lead to knowing important things that other people didn't.

If I was managing smaller money I'd be looking in smaller places, I'd look for mispricing.

Success means being very patient, but aggressive when it's time. And the more hard lessons you can learn vicariously rather than through your own hard experience, the better.

For each of us, really good investment opportunities aren't going to come along too often and won't last too long, so you've got to be ready to act and have a prepared mind.

I don't know anyone who learned to be a great investor with great rapidity.

Warren has gotten to be one hell of a lot better investor over the period I've known him, so have I. So the game is to keep learning.

You gotta like the learning process.

But I'd inject one line of caution: there's an apocryphal story about Mozart.

A 14-year-old came to him and said, "I want to learn to be a great composer." And Mozart said, "You're too young." The young man replied, "But I'm 14 years old and you were only eight or nine when you started composing."

To which Mozart replied, "Yes, but I wasn't running around asking other people how to do it."

Warren said that he often tells business school students that if he gave them a card that only had 20 punches for a lifetime, and each time they made an investment they would use up one punch, and that after 20 punches there would be no more, then on average, with those rules, you'll die a lot richer.

But people can't grasp this -- they don't know what to make of it. But I believe it's true -- you'll do better over a lifetime.

There are fewer opportunities than when I was young. Back then, we had just come out of a depression. Capitalism was a bad word. There had been abuses in the 1920s.

A joke going around then was the guy who said, *I bought stock for my old age and it worked — in six months, I feel like an old man.*

It's tougher for you, but that doesn't mean you won't do well — it just may take more time. But what the heck, you may live longer.

I think the people who tend to get the best results are these fanatics who just keep searching for the great businesses.

And the best of them don't expect to find ten, twenty or thirty.

They find one or two.

That's the right way to do it. And that's all you need are one or two.

I know the guy who invests with the banker that backed the Costco copy which was Home Depot. He also backed Eli Lilly very early.

He has several billion dollars between those two investments. He didn't need any more. In a lifetime of investment banking, that's what he got is two.

I regard that as a successful life. That isn't what they teach in our educational institutions.

They think it's some mystery they can teach that will make you better at investing. It's total bullshit.

There's no way to know enough about a thousand different stocks to be very good at it.

SEIZE THE OPPORTUNITY

This is one of the dumbest investment decisions I ever made.

After I wound up the partnership, I was a well to do fellow. I had enough so I didn't really have to work but I didn't have enough so I could do any damn thing I pleased.

A guy called me offering 300 shares of Belridge Oil and I had the cash and I said, "Sure, I'll take the listing."

In those days, Belridge was a pink-sheet company. It was very valuable. It had a huge oil field, it wasn't even leased, they owned everything, they owned the land, they owned the oil field, everything.

It had a liquidating value way higher than the per share price — maybe three times. It was just an incredible oil field that was going to last a long time, and it had very interesting secondary and tertiary recovery possibilities and they owned the whole field to do whatever they wanted with it. That's rare, too.

It was selling there maybe a fifth of what the oil companies were. They owned the oil field. So I bought it. Then he called me back and said, "I've got 1,500 more."

I didn't have the money on hand. I had to sell something. I think about it and I said, "hold it for 10 minutes and I'll call you back." I thought about it for 10 minutes and called him back and didn't buy it.

Well, Belridge Oil sold about for 35 times the price I was going to pay within a year and a half.

If I had made a different decision, the Mungers would be ahead by way of more than a billion dollars, as I sit here now.

To count the opportunity cost, it was a real boneheaded decision. There was no risk. I could have borrowed. It was a time when I had some pain from past borrowings.

The worst that would happen was I would get out with a small profit. It was a really dumb decision.

The stock was not overpriced because it was just a little more inconvenient for me to buy it. But the inconvenience was enough to trigger my mind.

The man who dominated the corporation was eccentric and heavy-drinking. But the oilfield wasn't over-drinking. I had two different psychological reasons so I made the wrong decision. I thought too much about how much the man was drinking and too little about how good the oilfield was. I thought too much about my inconvenience and too little about the basic situation.

You don't get that many great opportunities in a lifetime.

When life finally gave me one, I blew it. So I tell you that story to say you're no different from me.

You're not going to get that many really good ones. Don't blow your opportunities.

They're not that common, the ones that are clearly recognizable with virtually no downside and big upsides. Don't be too timid when you really have a cinch.

Go at life with a little courage. There's an old word commonly used in the south that I never hear anybody use now, except myself, and that's gumption.

I would say what you need is intelligence plus gumption.

GETTING RICH

We get these questions a lot from the enterprising young.

It's a very intelligent question -- you look at some old guy who's rich and you ask, *How can I become like you, except faster?*

My answer is that I did it slowly, inch by inch, taking losses mentally when they occurred.

If you want to do it with fast rapidity, then you're talking to the wrong man, but I know my way works.

Spend each day trying to be a little wiser than you were when you woke up. Discharge your duties faithfully and well. Step by step you get ahead, but not necessarily in fast spurts. But you build discipline by preparing for fast spurts. You may not need Zsa Zsa Gabor or a Lamborghini or a lot of other things you think you need now.

Slug it out one inch at a time, day by day, at the end of the day — if you live long enough — most people get what they deserve.

It's so simple.

PARI-MUTUEL BETTING

The model I like — to sort of simplify the notion of what goes on in a market for common stocks — is the pari-mutuel system at the racetrack.

If you stop to think about it, a pari-mutuel system is a market. Everybody goes there and bets and the odds change based on what's bet. That's what happens in the stock market. Any damn fool can see that a horse carrying a light weight with a wonderful win rate and a good post position etc. is way more likely to win than a horse with a terrible record and extra weight and so on and so on.

But if you look at the odds, the bad horse pays 100 to 1, whereas the good horse pays 3 to 2. Then it's not clear which is statistically the best bet using the mathematics of Fermat and Pascal.

The prices have changed in such a way that it's very hard to beat the system. And then the track is taking 17% off the top.

So not only do you have to outwit all the other betters, but you've got to outwit them by such a big margin that on average, you can afford to take 17% of your gross bets off the top and give it to the house before the rest of your money can be put to work.

Given those mathematics, is it possible to beat the horses only using one's intelligence? Intelligence should give some edge, because lots of people who don't know anything go out and bet lucky numbers and so forth. Therefore, somebody who really thinks about nothing but horse performance and is shrewd and mathematical could have a very considerable edge, in the absence of the frictional cost caused by the house take.

Unfortunately, what a shrewd horseplayer's edge does in most cases is to reduce his average loss over a season of betting from the 17% that he would lose if he got the average result to maybe 10%. However, there are actually a few people who can beat the game after paying the full 17%.

I used to play poker when I was young with a guy who made a substantial living doing nothing but bet harness races. Now, harness racing is a relatively inefficient market. You don't have the depth of intelligence betting on harness races that you do on regular races. What my poker pal would do was to think about harness races as his main profession. And he would bet only occasionally when he saw some mispriced bet available. And by doing that, after paying the full handle to the house — which I presume was around 17% — he made a substantial living. You have to say that's rare. However, the market was not perfectly efficient.

And if it weren't for that big 17% handle, lots of people would regularly be beating lots of other people at the horse races. It's efficient, yes. But it's not perfectly efficient. And with enough shrewdness and fanaticism, some people will get better results than others.

You're looking for a mispriced gamble. That's what investing is. And you have to know enough to know whether the gamble is mispriced. That's value investing.

You should remember that good ideas are rare. When the odds are greatly in your favor, bet heavily.

EMPIRES

The failure rate of great empires in terms of geography is 100%.

Just look at Athens and Britain today—everyone has passed the baton in due course. However, there is one sense in which these empires are still with us today. What was great about ancient Greece is with us in the world today—it has just moved.

You can be confident that the US will not be the most dominant and admired country in the world forever. We may have a longer run than most– we may even have a
long run ahead. But, we will eventually fall from the top.

But, the US has had a huge, constructive influence on Asia. Asia is important for the future of the world and many people there have learned from the US's experiences. Another person who has been a great instructor to the world is Lee Kwan Yew of Singapore. He helped change China. Where did Lee Kwan Yew learn his values? He was educated in England and was English speaking all of his life. As such, a lot of the culture of this room was absorbed by Singapore. If China becomes the greatest nation in the world, some of our best virtues will be a part of that country as well.

CULTIVATE LEARNING

The game of life is the game of everlasting learning. At least, it is if you want to win.

Develop into a lifelong self-learner through voracious reading. Cultivate curiosity and strive to become a little wiser every day.

Spend each day trying to be a little wiser than you were when you woke up. Day by day, and at the end of the day-if you live long enough-like most people, you will get out of life what you deserve.

I constantly see people rise in life who are not the smartest, sometimes not even the most diligent, but they are learning machines. They go to bed every night a little wiser than they were when they got up and boy does that help, particularly when you have a long run ahead of you.

In my whole life, I have known no wise people (over a broad subject matter area) who didn't read all the time -- none, zero.

You'd be amazed at how much Warren reads -- and at how much I read. My children laugh at me. They think I'm a book with a couple of legs sticking out.

If you don't keep learning, other people will pass you by.

Warren is one of the best learning machines on this earth. The turtles who outrun the hares are learning machines. If you stop learning in this world, the world rushes right by you.

Temperament alone won't do it - you need a lot of curiosity for a long, long time.

Acquire worldly wisdom and adjust your behavior accordingly.

If your new behavior gives you a little temporary unpopularity with your peer group, then to hell with them.

CIVILIZATION

Most of modernity came in the last 100 years. And the previous 100 years, there was some modernity. And then before that, things were pretty much the same for thousands of years.

Life in those years was brutal and short, there was no printing press, no AC, no modern medicine.

In the 100 years to 1922, you got the steam engine, steam ship, railroads, improvement in plumbing & improvement in farming.

In the next 100 years, you got widely distributed electricity, modern medicine, automobile, airplane, movies, AC, etc.

If you wanted 3 children back in the days, you needed to have 6 because half died in infancy. That's what our ancestors had to go through. Think of the agony they had to go through.

It's amazing how much achievement there's been in the last few hundred years and most of it has been in the last 100 years.

Now the trouble is all of the basic needs are filled and the principle problem of poor people in the US is that they're too fat. In the past, they're on the edge of starving.

All of these enormous increases in living standards, freedom, racial equality and all the huge progress that's come, people are less happy about state of affairs now than when things were way tougher.

ENVY

The world is not driven by greed. It's driven by envy.

The fact that everyone's five times better than they use to be -- they take that for granted. All they think about is that someone else has more now and they don't.

That's the reason God told Moses that you can't envy your neighbor's wife or even his donkey.

Even the old Jews were having troubles with envy so it's built into human nature.

I can't change the fact that a lot people are very unhappy and feel very abused after everything has improved by six hundred percent because there's still somebody else that has more.

I have conquered envy in my own life. I don't envy anybody else anymore. I don't give a damn what somebody else has.

But other people are going crazy by it.

I like the people who are against envy, not the people who are trying to profit from it.

Who in the hell needs Rolex watches just so you can get mugged for it?

Yet everyone wants to have a pretentious expenditure and that helps drive demand in our modern capitalist society.

My advice for young people is don't go there. I don't think there's much happiness in it.

Steven Pinker constantly points out how everything has gotten way, way better but the general feeling of how fair it is has gotten way more hostile.

As it gets better and better, people are less and less satisfied.

That is weird, but that's what has happened.

SELF-PITY

Self-pity gets pretty close to paranoia, and paranoia is one of the very hardest things to reverse. You do not want to drift into self-pity.

I have a friend who carried a big stack of index cards about this thick, and when somebody would make a comment that reflected self-pity, he would take out one of the cards, take the top one off the stack and hand it to the person, and the card said, "Your story has touched my heart, never have I heard of anyone with as many misfortunes as you".

Well, you can say that's waggery, but I suggest that every time you find you're drifting into self-pity, I don't care what the cause — your child could be dying of cancer — self-pity is not going to improve the situation.

Just give yourself one of those cards. It's a ridiculous way to behave, and when you avoid it, you get a great advantage over everybody else because self-pity is a standard condition and yet you can train yourself out of it.

CHINA

China is a big modern nation, it's got this huge population, and huge modernity that's come in the last 30 years.

Deng Xiaoping had to give up his own communist ideology to do something that worked better (e.g. ditching collectivist agriculture that led to a 60% boost in grain production). You don't see the Catholic Cardinal suddenly deciding there's no afterlife. But that's what Deng Xiaoping did. He gave up his ideology to make the economy work better.

He called it communism with Chinese characteristics. He meant one party government but with most of the property in private hands and a fair amount of free enterprise.

It's a marvelous thing he did for China and I think he will go down in history as one of the greatest leaders that any nation ever had. He brought that whole nation out of poverty and into prosperity over the course of 30 years after he made that decision. It's just amazing how well capitalism has served the Chinese.

We invested some money in China because we could get more value in terms of the strength of the enterprise and the price of the security than we could get in the US. Other people including Sequoia Capital have made the same decision we have.

The reason I invested in China is because I can get so much better companies at so much lower prices and I was willing to take a little political risk to get into the better companies at the lower prices. Other people might reach the opposite conclusion.

The Chinese government is worrying capitalists all around the world way more than it use to. Of course we don't like that.
We wish China and the US got along better. If you think about it, it's massively stupid that both nations have allowed tensions to rise.

If we make good friends out of the Chinese and vice versa, no other nations would bother us.

My generation after World War II, we took our enemies and made them our best friends (Germany & Japan). That was a real achievement.

Of course we should learn to get along with countries that have different systems of government. We like our government because we're use to it and it has the advantages of personal freedom.

But this wouldn't have worked for China. China wouldn't be in the position they're currently in and they did what they had to using their methods. We shouldn't be criticizing China because they're having terrible problems and they're not just like the US. China does some things better than we do. They should like us and we should like them.

Nothing is crazier than people who are fomenting resentments on either side.

ALIBABA

When you buy Alibaba, you do get a derivative (variable interest entity) but assuming there's a reasonable honor among civilized nations, ownership risk doesn't seem all that big to me.

Warren Buffett didn't invest in Alibaba because he doesn't feel as comfortable with the Chinese. It's a minor difference. I have all kinds of things where I'm just like Warren and I have all kinds of things where I'm not as comfortable as Warren and I just don't go near them. I think an old guy's entitled to invest where he wants to.

I don't think Alibaba is as entrenched as something like Alphabet or Apple. I think the internet is going to be a very competitive place even if you're a big internet retailer

APPLE

I think Apple is one of the strongest companies in the world.

I judge the strength of the company based on how much the customers love it.

And I've got zillions of friends who would almost part with their right arm before they part with their iPhone.

That's a hugely powerful position to be in.

I think Apple is one of the strong companies and will stay a strong company and I think it's un-Godly well managed.

JAPAN

Japan bought back not only their own debt but their common stocks. They haven't had inflation and they are still an admirable civilization.

They've been in stasis for 25 years with living standards not improving that much but I don't think that's the result of macroeconomic policies but a result of the rise in tough competition from China and South Korea.

It's encouraging that Japan can print as much money as they have and remain as civilized, admirable and calm as they have.

I hope US will have similar happy outcome but I think the Japanese are better adapted for stasis.

It's a duty-filled civilized bunch of people, most of them older, and they just suck it in and cope.

In US, we have terrible tensions and it's harder to run a country that's not mono-ethnic.

It's way harder to run country like US with different ethnicities and groups as oppose Japan which is mono-ethnic.

SINGAPORE

The best example in the whole world is probably Singapore which has zero debt, and never prints money and spends it.

It's one of the most successful places on Earth. I wish we were like that but there's only one Singapore.

I'd like to move some of Singapore's results to the United States. They have practically no deaths from opioids, they have a low crime rate, they have no debt in the whole country, they're doing a lot right.

Who's the one man that did the most for China? It was Lee Kuan Yew of Singapore. They copied him.

NEWSPAPERS

Each newspaper, all those local monopolies, was an independent bastion of power. The economic position was so impregnable, they were raw monopolies. The ethos of the journalists was to try and tell it like it is.

They were really a branch of the government. They call them the fourth estate meaning the fourth branch of the government. It arose by accident. Now about 95% of them have disappeared forever.

And what do we get in substitute? We get a bunch of people who attract an audience because they're crazy. I have my favorite crazies and you have you favorite crazies and we get together and we all become crazier as we hire people to tell us what we want to hear.

This is no substitute for Walter Cronkite and all those great newspapers of yesteryear. We have suffered a huge loss here.

It's nobody's fault -- it's just the creative destruction of capitalism. But it's a terrible thing that's happened to our country.

CRYPTOS

Crypto is like some venereal disease and beneath contempt.

I don't think it's good that our country is going crazy over Bitcoin and its ilk.

Some people think it's modernity and they welcome a currency that's so useful in extortions, kidnappings, tax evasion and so on.

And of course, with the envy, everybody has to create their own new currency. I think that's crazy too.

I wish cryptos had been banned immediately.

I admire the Chinese for banning it. I think they were right and we were wrong for allowing it.

In my life, I try and avoid things that are stupid, and evil and maybe look bad in comparison to somebody else. Bitcoin does all three.

In the first place, it's stupid because it's very likely to go to zero.
In the second place, it's evil because it undermines the Federal Reserve system and the national currency system which we desperately need to maintain its integrity and control and so on.

And third, it makes us look foolish compared to the communist leader in China. He was smart enough to ban Bitcoin in China.

With all of our presumed advantages of civilization, we are a lot dumber than the communist leader of China.

SPECULATION & GAMBLING

We have computers with algorithms trading against other computers.

We've got people who know nothing about stocks being advised by stock brokers who know even less. It's an incredibly crazy situation.

It's weird that we ever got a system where all of this equivalent of casino activity is all mixed up with a lot of legitimate long term investment. I don't think any wise country would have wanted this outcome.

Why would you want your country's stocks to trade on a casino basis to people that are just like the people that play craps and roulette at the casino. I mean it's crazy but it happened.

The great short squeeze on Gamestop was wretched excess.

The stock market has become a gambling parlor for many.

Everybody loves it because everyone's getting drunk at the party and they don't think about the consequences.

If I were a benign dictator, I would make it unfeasible to make short term gains on securities.

We don't need this wretched excess and it has bad consequences for this country.

You can argue that the wretched excess of the 1920s gave us the Great Depression, and the Great Depression gave us Adolf Hitler. This is serious stuff.

We have a liquid stock market which is two things at once — it's a place for people who are doing long-term investment rationally to go and make their transactions. And it's a place for another bunch of people to do casino gambling.

We mix them up totally. It's an absolutely insane thing for the country.

It would work a lot better if we didn't mix it up. It's like we mixed up running the Army with child prostitution or something. It's ludicrously crazy.

But that's what we did, and everybody that's making money out of it loves it this way.

The Poker tournaments are fashionable. People love this craze for for poker now and the bridge tournaments.

The gambling instinct is really strong. People love gambling and the trouble with it is, it's like taking heroin.

A certain percentage of people, when they start, just overdo it. It's that addictive.

It's crazy what we ended up with. It's absolutely crazy.

Civilization would have it a lot better without it.

Now we do get a certain amount of craziness in real estate, which doesn't have a liquid market.

It isn't like you wouldn't have a lot of excesses or speculation even if the stock markets were illiquid as real estate, but it wouldn't be as bad as it is now. Now it's gone beserk.

What Earthly good is it for our country to make the casino part of capitalism more and more efficient and more and more seductive? It's an insane public policy.

On the other hand, I think the chances of changing it are practically zero.

GAMING

Gaming is here to stay.

But then again, I'm an old man and I don't like the idea of addicted young men 40 hours per week playing games on TV.

It does not strike me as a good result for civilization.

I don't like anything which is so addictive you practically give up everything else to do it.

MARGIN DEBT

Well, of course, if you invest in marketable securities, you have the risk that they'll go down, you'll lose money instead of making it.

But if you hold a depreciating currency that's losing purchasing power, on balance we prefer the risk we have to those we're avoiding.

And we [at The Daily Journal] don't mind a tiny little bit of margin debt.

INFLATION

We've done something fairly extreme and don't know what the troubles will be but we are flirting with serious trouble. Some of our earlier fears were overblown though.

If you print too much money, you'll eventually cause terrible trouble. We're closer to terrible trouble than we've been in the past. But we may still be a long way off. I certainly hope so.

The solution that's the easiest for the politicians and the Federal Reserve is just to print more money and solve their temporary problems that way. That of course is going to have some long term dangers.

We know what happened in Germany when the Weimar Republic just kept printing money -- the whole thing blew up and that was a contributor to the rise of Hitler, a dictator hell-bent on war.

And Germany was a very advanced and civilized nation when Hitler took over. Little Albert Einstein, little Jewish boy, got his entire primary education with the insistence of the Catholic Church in Germany. Now that is very a civilized nation.

So if you let your nation deteriorate too much, what you get is a Hitler.

You could argue that [inflation] is the way democracies die.
All of this stuff is dangerous and serious and we don't want to

have a bunch of politicians just doing whatever is easy on the theory that it didn't hurt us last time so we can double it and do it one more time.

And then we double it again, and so forth. We know what happens on that everlasting doubling -- you will have a very different government if you keep on doing that enough. You're flirting with danger there somewhere unless there's some discipline in the process.

I predict our current politicians will not permit a new Volcker.

The conditions that allowed Volcker to tighten in the 1970s was very unusual without interference from the politicians.

All of the Latin American countries that printed too much money got a strongman.

If you look at the Roman Republic, they inflated their currency steadily for hundreds of years, and eventually the whole damn Roman Empire collapsed.

So it's the biggest long range danger we have probably, apart from nuclear war.

The safe assumption for an investor is that over the next hundred years, the currency is going to zero. That's my working hypothesis.

THE GREAT DEPRESSION ERA

The Great Depression was very formative for Munger who experienced those difficult years as a child.

Of course it was an advantage to see the Great Depression.

There had never been a depression that long in the civilized world. It just didn't go away.

It had fluctuations, but basically we went into the Great Depression, they threw everything at it that they thought they knew how to throw at it, and it just stayed there.

And the only thing that finally cured it was World War II.

The really interesting case was Germany. Germany had wiped out the currency in the Weimar inflation following World War I and created vast hardship.

When Hitler came in with his crazy paranoia and wanted to re-arm and so on, he created this artificial Keynesianism.

Germany, despite having botched its currency, by the time 1938 came about, Germany was the powerhouse of Europe.

The accidental Keynesianism of Adolf Hitler had restored Germany.

The new Reichsmark that Hitler created — it was spent like crazy on war preparation but that made it a very strong currency.

CAPITALISM'S TENDENCY

I think if we hadn't intervened [in the Global Financial Crisis] the way we did, which we've never done on this scale before, we might have had one of the most unholy financial messes.

We were headed for something that was going to try and become the Great Depression.

What they do is they feed on themselves.

The process of capitalism automatically speeds up in both booms and depressions, and it feeds on itself for a while.

It's like autocatalysis in chemistry — it's just automatic.

You get this speed up in both directions which makes it very, very dangerous.

Not just for the individual investors but for the whole civilization.

I am not being casual when I say that Adolf Hitler's rise came in part because of the Great Depression.

He never would have been Chancellor of Germany without that.

The Great Depression came from excesses which in many ways aren't as bad as those we have now.

FUND MANAGERS

Can you imagine an ordinary investment management firm saying, "We don't mind going down 30%"?

They'd be in terror or they would all be fired.

That means that 95% of the big-time national investing — they're closet indexers.

That is a deep moral compromise driven by incentives that none of us can do anything about.

It's almost as ridiculous as having a stock market that's also a gambling parlor.

And they can't avoid it. The university endowment officers also have to be closet indexers by the standards of the university endowment. The incentives are driving it.

You take the modern system of investment, I would say the modern big time investment banking has shifted into the shadow banks and other forms of private equity. They're just so huge and it's so much money and so much wealth being created.

It drives people crazy because you want to get in on it and so it gets bigger and bigger — but there's a lot of closet indexing in that too. They all want to do the same thing.

DIVERSIFICATION

The Mungers have Berkshire stock, Chinese stock, Costco stocks, Daily Journal stocks, and a bunch of apartment houses.

Do I think it's perfect?

No.

Do I think it's okay?

Yes.

You don't need all this damn diversification.

That's plenty. If you're trying to do better than average, you're lucky if you've got four good things to buy.

Twenty is really asking for egg in your beer. Very few people have enough brain to get twenty good investments.

ANTITRUST

I like the fact that we have strong national champions.

I think what's happened is so important and so tied up with national strength, I'm not trying to weaken the internet companies of the US.

I think other nations are proud of their big and strong companies too.

I don't think bigness is bad.

I don't want the whole of the internet to be dominated by foreign companies.

I want big strong American companies that stand well in the world.

So I'm not as worried about antitrust aspects of the internet.

ENERGY

We've got a lot of renewable energy we can get from solar and the wind. It's gotten efficient and competitive.

I'm in favor of conserving hydrocarbons instead of using them up as fast as possible. I'm in favor of all this new generating capacity now that it's gotten so efficient from solar and wind.

If there were no global warming problem, I would still do exactly what the government is now doing which is encouraging a hell of a lot more solar and wind. It would be smart to legislate the conservation of petroleum.

Petroleum has enormous chemical uses in fertilizers, chemistry, and so on. It's precious stuff and our national treasure. If it remains in the ground, it's a good place to store it.

I love the idea of conserving our natural resources. They're all going to be used up eventually. I'm in no hurry to use them up rapidly.

I like having big reserves of oil. I would just leave most of the oil we have here and I would pay whatever the Arabs charge for their oil and I would pay for it cheerfully and conserve my own. I think it's going to be very precious stuff over the next 200 years. Nobody else has my view and that doesn't both me because they're all wrong.

That is a very unusual attitude but it's mine.

If you stop to think about it, the oil industry has been so vilified now, I can hardly think of a more useful industry. I don't know about wildcatters but certainly the petroleum engineers I know and the people who design our oil refineries and pipelines are some of the finest and most reliable people I know.

And I see very little trouble with the oil supply thing in the United States. So I'm basically in love with Standard Oil and I don't have this feeling that it's an evil, crazy place. I wish the rest of the world worked as well as our big oil companies.

And China has the correct solution. Imported oil is not your enemy, it's your friend.

Every barrel that you use up that comes from somebody else is one less barrel of your precious oil which you're going to need to feed your people and maintain your civilization.

And what responsible people do with a Confucius ethos is they suffer now to benefit themselves, their families, and their countrymen later. And the way to do that is to go very slow on producing your own oil.

You want to produce just enough so that you keep up on all of the technology.

And don't mind at all paying prices that look ruinous for foreign oil. It's going to get way worse later. Every barrel of foreign oil that you use up instead of using up your own — you're going to eventually realize you were doing the right thing.

I think that it's partly the economists who have caused the problem.

Because they have this theory that if people react in a free market that it's much better than any type of government planning but there is a small class of problems where it's better to think the things through in terms of the basic science and ignore these signals from the market.

Now if I'm right in this, there are a whole lot of lessons that logically follow:

- Foreign oil is your friend not your enemy
- You want to produce your own assets slow
- The oil in the ground you're not producing is a national treasure

Running out of hydrocarbons is like running out of civilization.

All this trade, all these drugs, fertilizers, fungicides, etc. which China needs to eat with a population so much, they all come from hydrocarbons.

And it is not at all clear that there is any substitute.

When the hydrocarbons are gone, I don't think the chemists will be able to simply mix up a vat and there will be more hydrocarbons.

It's conceivable of course that they could but it's not the way to bet.

GLOBAL WARMING

I'll be very surprised if it's as bad as people say it going to be.

The temperature of the earth went up 1 degree centigrade in about 200 years.

There was a hell of a lot of coal, oil that was burned and I'm just skeptical about whether it's as bad as these calamity howlers are saying.

COVID & VACCINE

If we get lucky, it'll fade away.

We kill 30,000 people with flu every year in the US.

Suppose we're at 60,000 and we included omicron. I think we get use to it.

I have been appalled by the fear of vaccination in the big chunk of the nation.

Speaking for myself, I couldn't wait to be vaccinated.

I think the risks of being vaccinated are way less than the risks of not being vaccinated. So it's really massively stupid not to welcome vaccination and we probably have 30% of the people in the country that think vaccination is evil and coming after them like the Hobgoblins.

It's not good that there's that much ignorance left.

If I were running the world, vaccinations would be mandatory.

When I was in World War II's army, they didn't ask me if I wanted a vaccination. They just vaccinated me.

That didn't hurt me or anybody else in that world.

We all just submitted to whatever the government told us to submit to. And it was no big deal.

I don't like big chunks of the country going crazy and I would argue that the anti-vaxxers are somewhat crazy.

It's just so much safer to be vaccinated than not vaccinated.

And so much more considerate to your fellow citizens.

It's a massive kind of ignorance that 30% of the people have.

THE GREAT RESIGNATION

The pandemic has made lots of people use to not going to the office 5 days a week and I think a lot of those people are never going back to that.

We overshot with the stimulus and making welfare so liberal by helicoptering this money out. It was hell to man the restaurants.

I think Larry Summers was quite possibly right, that we overshot. We would have been smart to do with a little less.

Capitalism works when able bodied young people feel agony if they refuse to work. It's because of that agony that this whole economic system works.

The only effective economies that we've had that brought us modernity and prosperity we now have, they imposed a lot of hardship on young people who didn't want to work.

You take away all the hardship and you say stay home and you get more than you get if you come to work, it's quite disruptive to an economic system like ours.

The next time we do this, I don't think we ought to be so liberal.

TIMING MARKETS

In my whole adult life I've never hoarded cash waiting for better conditions.

I've just invested in the best things that I can find and I'm not going to change now.

The Daily Journal has used up all of its cash.

Berkshire has lots of excess cash but not to time markets -- it's only because we can't find any investments with prices we're willing to pay.

HAPPINESS II

You don't have a lot of envy.

You don't have a lot of resentment.

You don't overspend your income.

You stay cheerful in spite of your troubles.

You deal with reliable people.

You do what you're supposed to do.

All of these simple rules work so well to make your life better. And they're so trite.

Can you be cheerful when you're absolutely mired in deep hatred and resentment? Of course you can't. So why would you take it on?

The secret to happiness is to lower your expectations -- that is what you compare your experience with.

Have realistic expectations which is low expectations.
You want to have reasonable expectations and take life's results, good or bad, as they happen with a certain amount of Stoicism.

There will never be a shortage of good people in the world.

All you need to is get as many as possible in your life and keep the rest the hell out.

MUNGER'S BOOK RECOMMENDATIONS

- Poor Charlie's Almanack
- Seeking Wisdom by *Peter Bevelin*
- Outliers by *Malcolm Gladwell*
- Consipiracy of Fools by *Kurt Eichenwald*
- The Martians of Science by *Istvan Hargittai*
- The Wealth and Poverty of Nations: Why Some Are So Rich and Some So Poor by *David Landes*
- The Path to Power, Means of Ascent, and Master of the Senate by *Robert Caro*
- Benjamin Franklin by *Walter Isaacson*
- Einstein by *Walter Isaacson*
- Les Schwab by *Les Schwab*
- Andrew Carnegie by *Joseph Frazier Wall*
- Titan by *Ron Chernow*
- John Adams by *David McCullough*
- How Scots Invented The Modern World by *Arthur Herman*
- The Selfish Gene by *Richard Dawkins*
- Three Scientists and Their Gods by *Robert Wright*
- Genome by *Matt Ridley*
- No Two Alike by *Judith Rich Harris*
- The Language Instinct by *Steven Pinker*
- Darwin's Blind Spot by *Frank Ryan*
- Influence by *Robert Cialdini*
- Faraday, Maxwell, and the Electromagnetic Field: How Two Men Revolutionized Physics by *Nancy Forbes and Basil Mahon*
- The Martians of Science by *Istvan Hargittai*
- Deep Simplicity: Bringing Order to Chaos and Complexity by *John Gribbin*
- Ice Age by *John Gribbin*
- Fiasco: The Inside Story of a Wall Street Trader by *Frank Partnoy*

- Conspiracy of Fools by *Kurt Eichenwald*
- Models of My Life by *Herbert A. Simon*
- A Matter of Degrees: What Temperature Reveals about the Past and Future of Our Species, Planet, and Universe by *Gino Claudio Segrè*
- Guns, Germs, and Steel: The Fates of Human Societies by *Jared Diamond*
- The Third Chimpanzee: The Evolution and Future of the Human Animal by *Jared Diamond*
- Getting It Done by *John Richardson and Roger Fisher*
- Fortune's Formula by *William Poundstone*
- Hard Drive: Bill Gates and the Making of the Microsoft Empire by *James Wallace*
- Distant Force: A Memoir of the Teledyne Corporation and the Man Who Created It, with an Introduction to Teledyne Technologies by *G. A. Roberts*
- The Outsiders: Eight Unconventional CEOs and Their Radically Rational Blueprint for Success by *William N. Thorndike, Jr.*

SUPER INVESTOR SERIES

The Super Investor Series is designed for curious people that want to expand their thinking through the perspectives and thoughts of highly intelligent investors.

Other books in the Super Investor Series:

- *The Almanack of Stanley Druckenmiller*
- *The Almanack of Michael Burry*
- *The Almanack of Jim Simons*
- *The Almanack of Jim Chanos*
- *The Almanack of Ed Thorp*
- *The Psychology of Misjudgment: A Workbook*

Bonus content available on SuperInvestorSeries.com

ALSO WRITTEN BY THE AUTHOR

51 Questions That Changed My Life: Tool for Self-Reflection

Knowledge Athlete : Outcompete In The Knowledge Economy By Learning Faster and Smarter

Printed in Great Britain
by Amazon